Curious Carter and the Real Super Heroes

Rose M G Jackson

Curious Carter and the Real Super Heroes
by Rose M G Jackson

Email: Rosejackson144@gmail.com

Www.rose-jackson@fineartsmerica.com

Features Drawings by Christopher Jones

In Memory of
Author Mary Wilson
and
Sister-in-law

Publishing
Sue Breeding
Creating-Design
P.O. Box 1785
Columbus, IN 47202

Meet Curious Carter.

He's always dreaming of being a super hero! In his dreams, he uses his magical powers to put bad guys to sleep while he gets the other kids to safety.

Curious Carter was born with several missing ribs from his spine. He lives just fine without them. He often dreams he is Kiyan the Super Hero.

Curious Carter enjoys playing with his younger sisters (Charlee and Nadia) and taking karate class.

When Curious Carter is not dreaming of becoming "Kiyan the Super Hero," he is playing games on his phone, playing with his sisters, and taking karate classes.

Often he finds himself making paper airplanes just like his Grandpop or playing with his best friend who also has the name Carter.

Meet Courageous Carter.

He has been Curious Carter's best friend since the first grade. He too is always dreaming of becoming a super hero!

In his dreams he gets his super powers from his special eyeglasses. The glasses allow him to see through anything, including brick walls. In his dreams he partners with his best friend Curious Carter to solve some elementary school problems.

When he is not using his imagination, he is playing with his brother Brad, and keeping his little sister Emily out of trouble.

Carter finally found the courage to face bully, after bully, after bully. They picked on him, because he was quiet and wore glasses.

While it was not a very easy thing to do, Courageous Carter did not let the bad kids see his fears. He asked and received support from his parents and teachers.

Courageous Carter's grandmother often told him stories about the amazing courage his grandfather and his grandfather's brother had as young men fighting in World War II.

This gave Courageous Carter the courage he needed to be brave.

As you can see, Curious Carter and Courageous Carter have much in common. Both boys love to imagine they are super heroes.

Their birthdays are in the month of March, they often make the honor roll, and the entire school thinks they are cool dudes.

The boys love being around their grandparents.

They do get in trouble at times. After all, they are kids with curious minds.

Some people call them the Carter boys.

Meet Dr. Darian.

Dr. Darian studied art and technologies receiving many honors in college. He teaches art therapy and science at the boys' school.

Middle school can be a tough time for kids. It is a time when everyone is trying to fit in. More importantly, some of the kids think they must have the same phones, clothes, and etc., as everyone else to fit in and this is clearly not the case. Especially now when everyone is facing this pandemic.

Dr. Darian uses his art classes to give students a chance to express their feelings about school peer pressures, sports, and current events such as the pandemic and race relationships.

Growing up, he loved hearing his grandmother Jan tell stories about his great-great grandfather who was the first African American Congressman in the Republican Party in 1889 in the state of North Carolina.

Dr. Darian believes he gets his love for the arts and people of all colors from his grandmother Jan.

Meet Major C.

Major C is a new kid at the school. He is having a terrible time fitting in. On the first day of school, he stole Dr. Darian's painting.

When asked about the painting, Major C did not tell the truth. First, he said Ashley did it, next he said Germain stole it. You must know that both Ashley and Germain are known for being bullies. However, using his special glasses, the boys found the painting in Major C's locker.

On the second day, Major C called a girl a terrible name and made her cry.

On day three, Major C was so upset with his math grades that he put his homework in the trashcan. He was acting out really, really, bad.

Seeing this, the Carter boys decided to invite the new kid to skate with them. They wanted to see if they could help Major C become a better person before things really got out of control.

Major's parents (The Coopers) were very happy the Carter boys wanted to spend time with their son. It was the last day of school and the last time the boys could play together without face coverings due to the pandemic for a few days. After a few minutes on the skates the three boys sat down to drink their water.

Curious Carter said to Major C, "You know, I was once the new kid in school. I was very angry and stayed mad all the time too. I threw things, I broke things, and was mad at the world because I needed a lot of surgeries and no one else did. I did not know how to control my feelings. One day my surgeon had a long talk with me. He told me the surgeries were needed because he wanted me to be the best kid I could be. The surgeries helped me to stand straight, run fast, play soccer, and take karate classes without any back pain."

Today, Dr. Otegen and I are best friends. He is my real super hero!" said Carter with excitement.

Meet Dr. Otegen

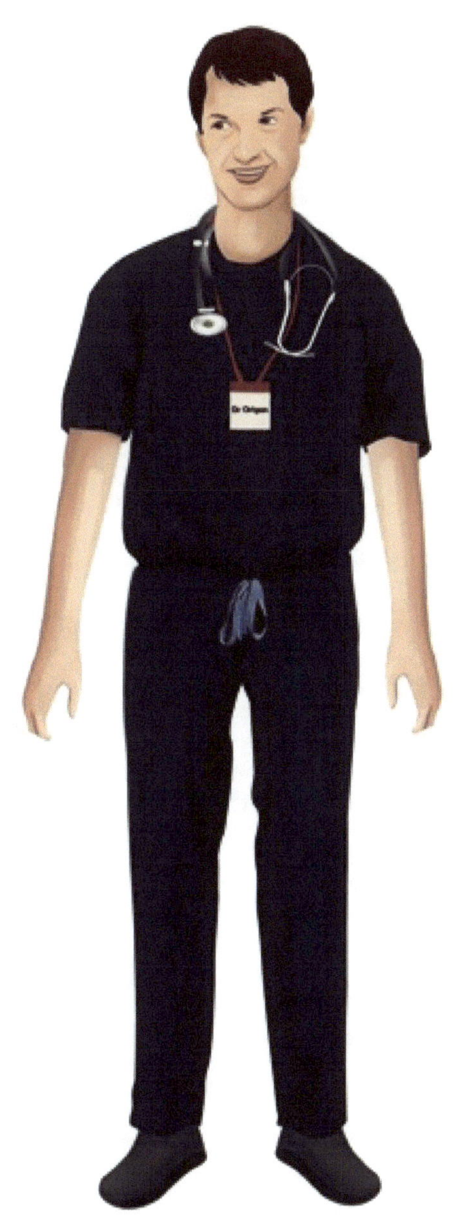

Can you believe I have had 20 surgeries already?" Curious Carter said.

"20!" Major C said in disbelief.

"Yes! It's true," Curious Carter said.

"So what happened to you?" Curious Carter asked.

Major C explained, "I just lost my best friend to this pandemic. I am so scared my entire family will die. Then we moved here. I don't have any friends now."

"Oooh! Wow!" both Carters replied.

The boys all gave Major a big hug by touching elbows. Major C began to feel much, much better after telling the boys about his feelings.

The boys asked Major C if he would like to be their friend. Major shouted with excitement.

"Yes! Yes! Yesss! I heard you boys were real super heroes! Can I be one too? People already say I look like the Curious Carter," Major C smiled.

Curious Carter and Courageous Carter looked at each other with a big smile and laughed.

Curious Carter said to Major, "Slow down, slow down! You, your family, and friends can all be real super heroes by just being kind to everyone."

Courageous Carter said, "Yes, my grandparents, my parents, and Dr. Darian are my superheros."

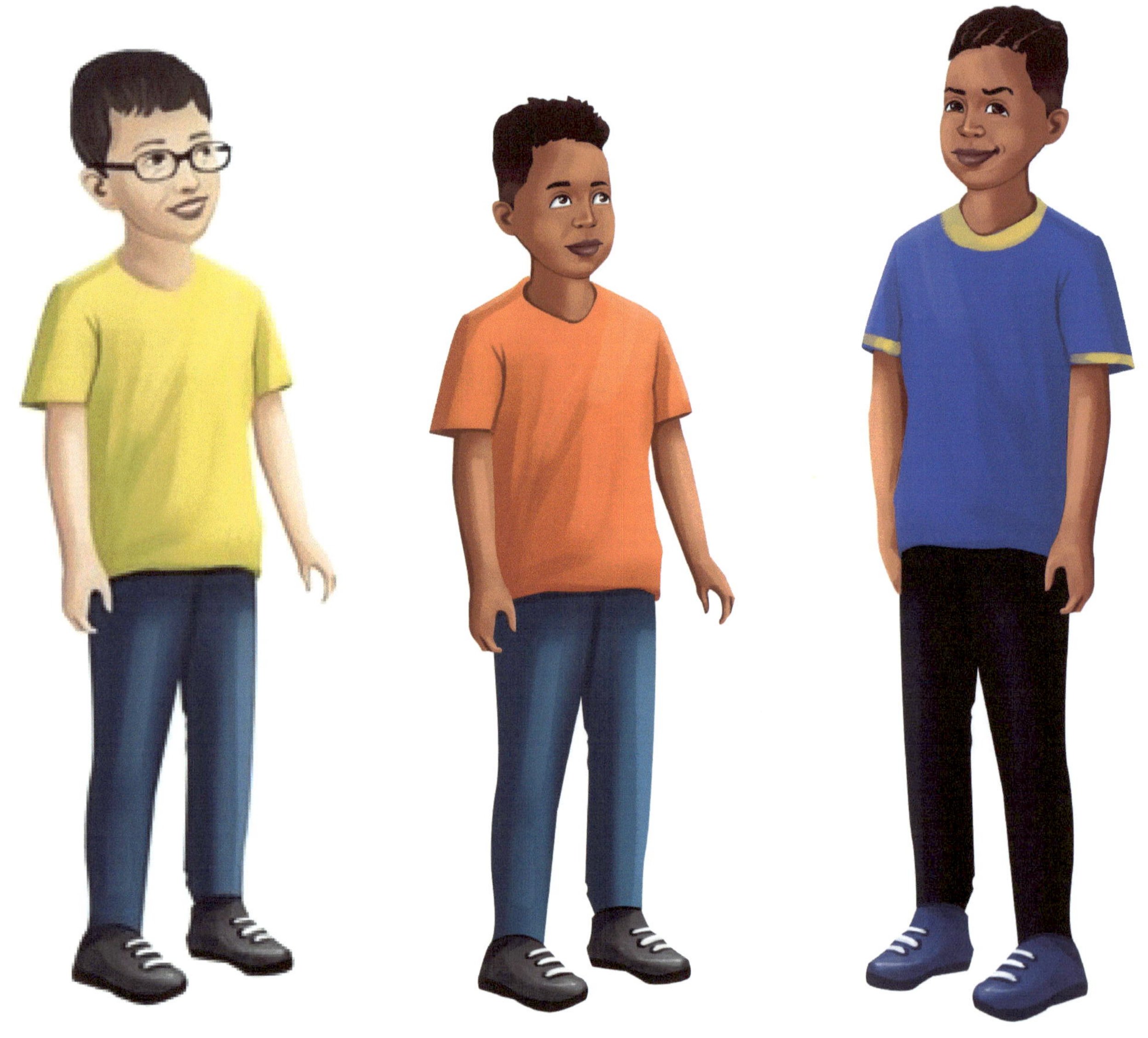

Secret Missions

"My great-grandfather lead secret missions against Germany back in the day. He was assigned to block their communications signals during the war. The United States would go on to win this war! So my grandmother said she knows we can defeat this COVID virus. We just have to be kind, wash our hands, eat better, stay home and be happy," Courageous Carter said with a big smile.

Curious Carter said, "My family, Dr. Otegen's team, and I have some very brave uncles (Al, Leroy, and Fred) who fought in some awful wars too. They are my real, real, real super heroes, and my dads!"

Music and Sickle Cells!

Curious Carter said, "Did you know our music teacher Mr. Green lives with pain, because his blood cells are shaped like sickles."

"A sickle," Major C said.

"Yes sickles," Courageous Carter said. "When Mr. Green was in school, he made the honor roll every year and his pain did not stop him from being nice to everyone. He chose not to be a bully, and that's the makings of a real super hero! He sure knows his music too!"

First Black Republican Elected to Congress in the 1880s!

"What about Dr. Darian's great-great-grand father? He was the only African American in the south elected to Congress a long, long, long time ago. I bet he was super, super, smart!" Curious Carter said.

My Maternal Grandfather. First African American Congressman from North Carolina.

politician, elected as a Republican member of the United States House of Representatives from 1889 to 1893 from North Carolina. He was one of only five African Americans elected to Congress from the South in the Jim Crow era of the last decade of the nineteenth century, as disfranchisement reduced black voting. After that, no African Americans would be elected from the South until 1972 and none from North Carolina until 1992.

Henry Plummer Cheatham

"Hey guys lets' make a Honor Roll Challenge. We must stay top students in all of our classes so we can be honor roll students like Mr. Green. I think we can do it!

What about you Major? I bet you can make the honor roll too! But you really must stop doing those terrible things. Stealing and acting out is just so wrong! When you're feeling upset just think about how you are hurting everyone. If it helps, just talk to us first.

We might not have all the answers but at least we can try," Curious Carter explained.

The boys all smiled and dabbed!

REPORT
CARD
Honor Roll
REPORT
CARD
Honor Roll

"Yeah, you are right," Major C said. "I have a lot of apologizing to do."

"I am so embarrassed. But it is worth it if I can be your friend and become a real super hero," Major C said with excitement.

Curious Carter laughs and says, "The Rose Garden!"

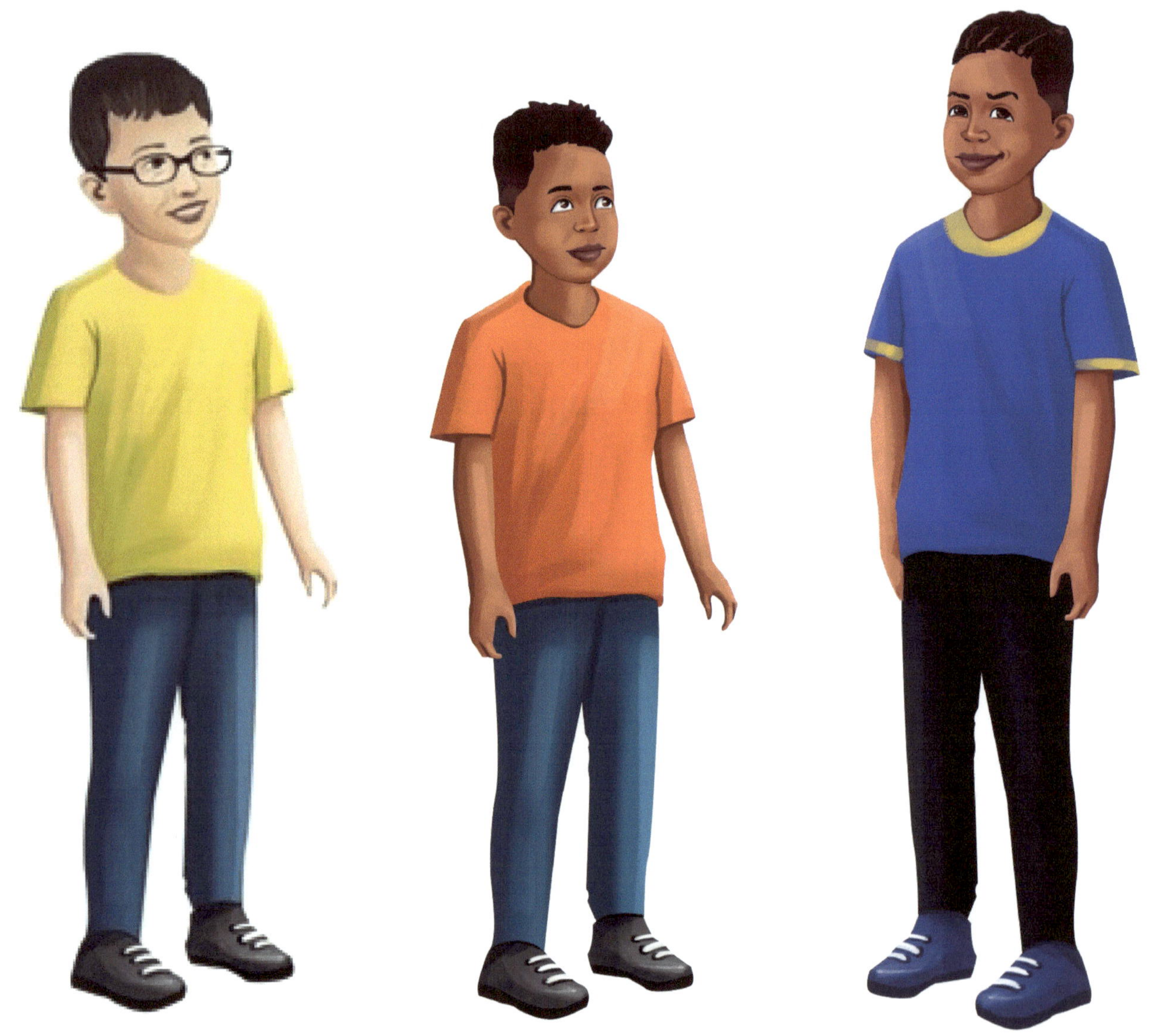

"Major C, I thought I was going to have to take you to my Grandma Rose. She made me take five yoga classes, just so I could learn how to center my mind and body. I had to learn how to walk away from fights. That yoga madness did work though. And! She made me pick hours of weeds out of her huge Rose Garden. It's the size of a football field," says Carter.

"Man! I'll tell you, you don't want to spend hours with my grandmother Rosie," says Carter.

Carter and the boys laugh.

Major C replied, "Man! I heard about your grandmother before I even moved to this neighborhood!"

Curious Carter said, "Yeah! She will make you wash your hands ten times before she gives you her famous chocolate veggie cookies. But, I have to say, they are delicioussss!"

Courageous Carter agreed!

The three boys skated off to their homes feeling good about their new friend Major C, and knowing they had real super heroes in their very own families.

Friends for Life!

The three boys would go on to graduate from Middle School and High School together. They each decided to go to different colleges. They made another challenge to get together every summer to check in on their favorite teachers Dr. Darian and Mr. Green.

Curious Carter studied medicine in hopes to find a cure for missing bones and the pandemic.

Courageous Carter studied space science in hopes to one day join the space program.

Major C studied behavioral awareness health and political science in hopes to help teens conquer their fears and manage stress on a national level.

Two Dawings by Christopher Jones
(Biological father of Curious Carter)

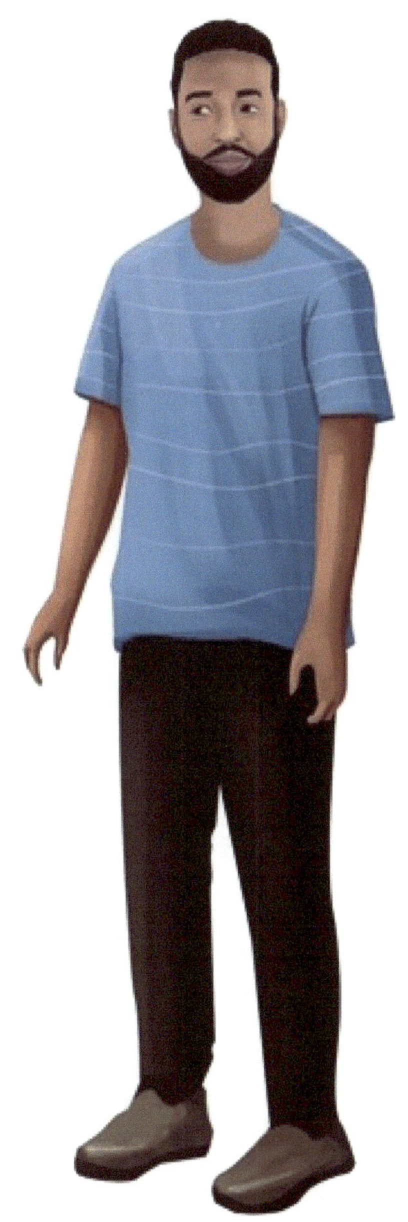

Coloring Book ….

The next pages in this book include some drawings of the real super heroes the boys spoke about in this story.

Can you color each of them?

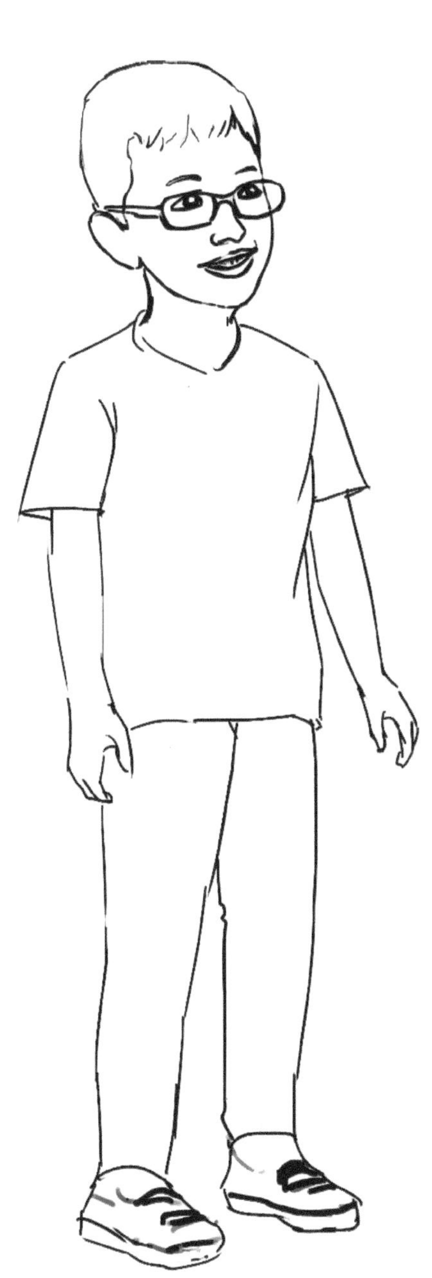 

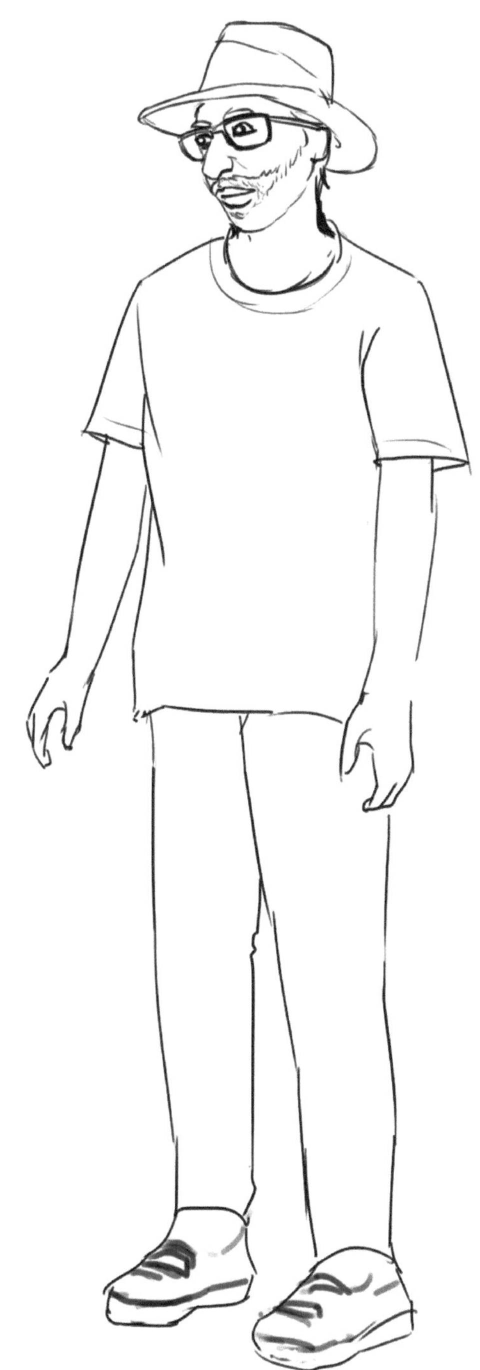

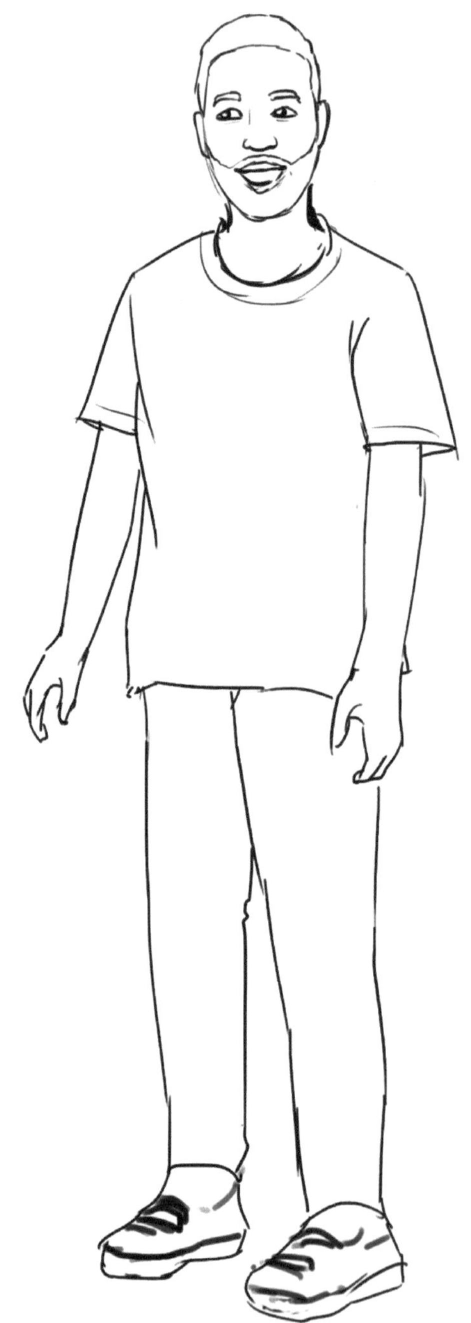

If you dreamed of being a super hero what would your superpowers be?

What would your name be?

Acknowledgements

Christopher Jones
Mrs. Janet B. Jones
Mrs. Denise Higgins
George T. Eley 3rd
Shirley S. Colden
Cortney R. Jackson
Carter K. Jackson
Johnetta Baugham
Gayla M. Williams
Caren Weldon
Emily Threat
Ocean M. Green
Wandra V. McKee
Rev. Michael McLeon
Rev. Robert Ford
Scooter Powell
Arnold Jackson
Calvin McNeil
Mary Wilson Family
Tony and Karen Jenkins

Special Thanks to
Mrs. Michelle Margaitis
Laura Margaitis
Karen Dobson Rheinhardt
Jaren Reheinhardt

Photos of Family and Friends

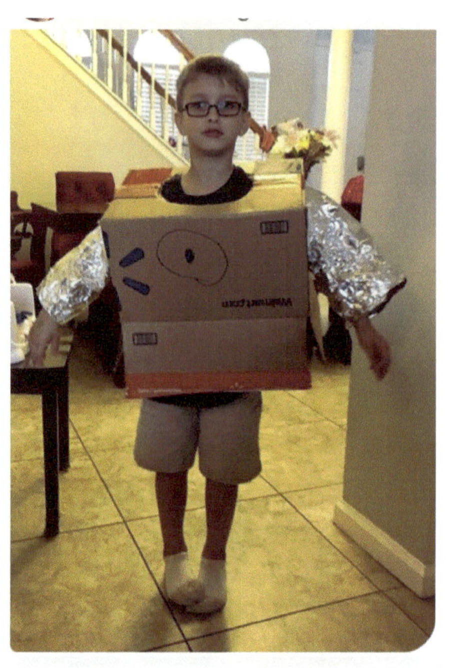

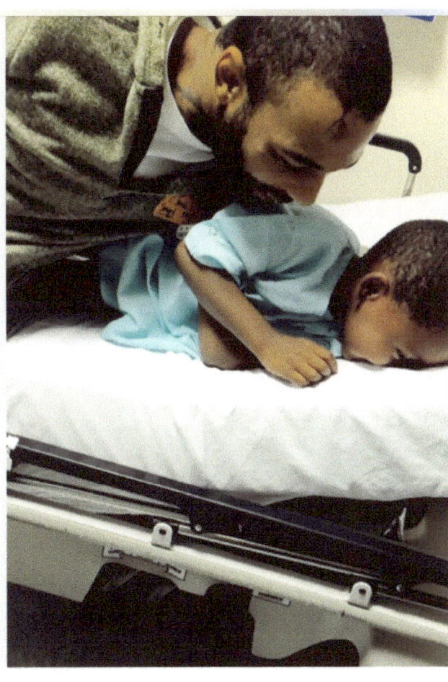

8.27.2019

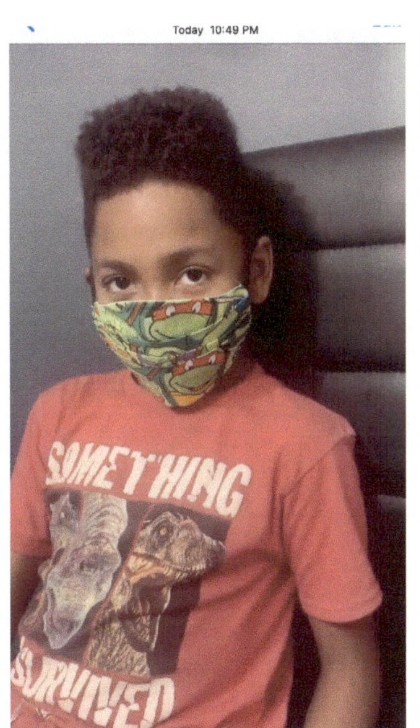

Thank you
Carter Jackson
7-2020